FLIGHT ON NEW WINGS

Also by Mary Willette Hughes

QUILT PIECES

Flight on New Wings

HEALING THROUGH POETRY

Mary Willette Hughes

NORTH STAR PRESS OF ST. CLOUD, INC.

Cover photograph © Myron Jay Dorf/CORBIS

Author photograph © Dianne Towalski/*St. Cloud Visitor*

ISBN: 0-87839-196-7

First Edition, April 2003

Printed in the United States of America
by
Versa Press, Inc.
East Peoria, Ilinois

Published by:
North Star Press of St. Cloud, Inc.
Post Office Box 451
St. Cloud, Minnesota 56302-0451

10 9 8 7 6 5 4 3 2 1

ACKNOWLEDGMENTS

The poems in *Flight on New Wings* have been read and critiqued by many poet-teachers, readers, and friends. Without their incisive suggestions, kind encouragement and generous friendship, this book could not have been completed. It has evolved over the last thirteen years, first as a book of poetry, and then as a poetry therapy book with a vision that it could be used in treatment programs for addiction.

I am deeply grateful to the following people:

Editor/consultant:
Geri Giebel Chavis, Ph.D., L.P., C.P.T., and poet

Readers and commentators:
Arleen McCarty Hynes, O.S.B., R.P.T.
Nancy Hynes, O.S.B., Ph.D., professor
Terry Hauptman, Ph.D., poet and artist
Alan Downes, Ph.D.
Claire van Breeman Downes, M.A., poet
Eva Hooker, C.S.C., Ph.D., professor, poet
Adella Espelien, Ph.D., R.N., specialty area, Psychiatric Nursing and Mental Health
Gretchen Swanson, M.A., poet

I wish to thank Bernard J. Belling, M.S.L.P., L.I.C.S.W., Clinical Services Coordinator of the Recovery Plus Unit at the St. Cloud Hospital for offering the opportunity to become a co-facilitator of poetry therapy and work with staff therapists.

I wish to thank Steve Lanz, M.S., L.I.S.W., who first read the poems and encouraged the meeting with Bernard Belling to initiate poetry therapy sessions which are now an integral part of the Recovery Plus program.

I wish to thank the staff therapists who co-facilitate the following groups with me:
Gordon D. Oettel, M.S. (men)
Loree Leroux, M.S. (women)
Molly Sveumm, M.S. (adolescents)
Lana Nienaber, B.A., C.G.C. (gamblers)
Robert Gruber, M.S., L.S.W., and June Huberty, R.N., C.C.D.P. (families)

I wish to thank North Star Press for publishing *Flight on New Wings*.

And I wish to thank my dear husband, Mark, who has encouraged the writing of this book and my work at Recovery Plus. His editorial skills are stellar.

dedication

to our son
and to all
who have survived
who have endured
who walk forward

TABLE OF CONTENTS

II. ADDENDUM

FOREWORD

One of our sons began using drugs and alcohol in the fifth grade. When he was sixteen, my husband and I committed him for evaluation and subsequent treatment at the St. Cloud Hospital in St. Cloud, Minnesota.

Research has shown that addiction may happen because a person is genetically prone to it, which may be true for our son since alcoholism exists on both sides of our families. A second influence may be a traumatic experience of helplessness at a young age. Dr. Drew Pinsky, a physician and specialist in addiction treatment and medical director of the Department of Chemical Dependency Services at Las Encinas Hospital in Pasadena, California, writes: "Many addicts have gone through some profound experiences of powerlessness in childhood," ("Your Family's Health," *Minneapolis Star Tribune Magazine*, June 3, 2001). Such an experience happened to our son.

Thirty-three years ago my husband and I and our seven children went on a weekend camping trip with a group of friends and their children. A seminarian from the St. Cloud Diocesan Seminary, a good friend of our friends, came along to enjoy the weekend, play with the kids and lead our prayer services. He was active in youth organizations and had spent overnight visits in our friends' homes. We trusted him.

It was considered an honor for one of the young boys to be chosen by the seminarian to spend Friday and Saturday nights in his tent. On Saturday, the seminarian asked if our six-year-old son could spend the night with him. We trusted him. We said yes.

At 5:00 A.M. the next morning, our son ran down the hill and into our tent screaming and crying that the man had hurt him. The seminarian had sexually abused our son.

We were dumbfounded, angry and sick at heart. We didn't know what to do. We packed up and left the campground Sunday, before the scheduled leaving time, while the seminarian led the rest of the group in a prayer service. My husband was livid; I was in shock; we felt utterly betrayed, but we did not confront the seminarian. In retrospect, it was a grave mistake that our son did not see us stand up for him against the seminarian, that he did not see or hear us validate his experience or acknowledge his feelings of anger and hurt. We simply wanted to leave and take our seven children home where they would be safe.

That Sunday night we took our son into our bed to talk to him about what had happened. I remember we told him the man who had hurt him was sick, but what does that really mean to a little child?

We never brought up the subject with our son again. We hoped he would forget it. We were wrong.

A licensed therapist, a friend of ours, was also on that camping trip. We made an appointment to see him on the Monday morning after the incident to discuss the situation. We kept the appointment with our therapist friend. My husband and I threatened to bring a lawsuit against the seminarian unless professional counseling for his problem was arranged. We also felt he should not become a priest. (Thirty-three years ago even this was a bold position.) At this point our therapist friend revealed that he had been counseling the seminarian for pedophilia. The therapist told us he knew the seminarian had chosen our son to be with him for the night but didn't say anything to warn us because he thought the seminarian was cured. We could hardly believe what he was telling us. We were betrayed again. The therapist's exact words were, "I gambled and lost." Our question, "Who lost?"

About twelve years ago our son told me how extremely angry he was that Sunday morning of the camping trip, particularly at his father for not "decking" the man who had abused him. He never knew about our visit to the therapist or our threat to bring a law suit against the seminarian. We didn't tell him then because we simply felt he was too young to understand.

Our son carried this anger against us through his early years in school. I believe his anger grew over the years because he felt that since we did nothing to defend him, we didn't care about him, and we thought he was bad. I believe these factors contributed greatly to his difficult personality and to his subsequent use of drugs and alcohol.

I now work as a co-facilitator of poetry therapy in the Recovery Plus adult program for addiction at the St. Cloud Hospital with a staff therapist present at each session. The poems used are from *Flight on New Wings* and were written as a result of our son's and our family's experiences. Recently my work as a co-facilitator has been expanded to one session a month with the adolescents, the family groups, and those suffering with a gambling addiction.

Our son has read most of the poems in *Flight on New Wings* and gives his permission to use them if they can help others, but they do not help him. He does not want to be reminded of the pain and suffering experienced in his early and adolescent years, but he does understand that writing the poems has been therapeutic for me, helping me to recover from the trauma that occurred. Though he is in his twenty-third year of recovery, his wound is still raw and a deep anger lives in him. He recently told me: "Some things you do not forget and cannot forgive, but you learn to live with them." At the present time he is receiving counseling. He has always been faithful in attending AA meetings, a lifeline for him, and they continue to be an important part of his life.

Most of the poems are poems of memory. Only the poem, "That Night," written in 1989, grew from an immediate crisis situation involving our son, a crisis I could not control, make better or resolve, but one that I could write about. After thirty-three years, some of the details of that camping weekend have blurred in my husband's and my memories, but the abuse that occurred is a reality that has had a life-long impact.

The poems deal with issues surrounding sexual abuse, addiction, as well as the process of recovery. Some of the incidents depicted in a few poems were generated from a wider knowledge of the world of addiction and not from direct experience. My hope is that these poems will speak for and to others and give a voice to those who have suffered similar experiences.

Although addiction does not always occur after a person experiences sexual abuse, it may occur. In the poetry therapy sessions at the hospital, some patients have disclosed the same journey as our son: after being sexually abused they also turned to drugs and alcohol. It is hoped that these poems contain universal experiences associated with abuse, addiction, and recovery. It is possible that recognition of other issues such as depression, suicide, battering, rejection may result from a discussion of a particular poem's content, as well as issues of hope, peace, joy, honesty, sobriety, and life after treatment.

Poetry therapy is usually an on-going experience over a specified period of time where the same participants attend several successive sessions. In Recovery Plus, where poetry therapy is a part of the treatment program, it occurs only once in the course of the patient's twenty-eight-day stay, a variant of the usual experience of poetry therapy.

The poems serve a therapeutic purpose in Recovery Plus and they can also provide this kind of experience in other treatment programs. Since January of 2000, nearly 500 people have been participants in poetry therapy sessions at the St. Cloud Hospital. From completed evaluations, the percentage indicating a positive experience has been approximately ninety percent for the women and eighty percent for the men . . . overall, an eighty-four percent positive response. Considering that attendance is mandatory, that patients' backgrounds are diverse and that the length of time patients have been in treatment is varied, (some are in the first days, others are ready to graduate) it appears from their viewpoint, that poetry therapy is helpful, a valid and valuable tool in their recovery program.

An addendum section follows the poem section of this book. It contains a definition of poetry therapy and its basic premise, the objectives of poetry therapy, and a suggested format for group sessions. Also, each poem has companion questions that may be used by therapists to elicit discussion or a written response. Finally, an evaluation form is also included which may be completed at the end of a session if that is desired by the therapist.

It is hoped that individuals who are not part of a clinical program may also find the poems and information included in the addendum helpful and enriching for their own personal healing and growth.

STATEMENT

Bernard J. Belling, M.S.L.P., L.I.C.S.W.
Clinical Services Coordinator
Recovery Plus Chemical Dependency Treatment Unit
St. Cloud Hospital
St. Cloud, Minnesota

Mary Willette Hughes has demonstrated the power of poetry with her poems collected under the title, *Flight on New Wings*.

Poetry, even though it is a verbal and written mode of communication, can provide a means of communicating on an intuitive and emotional level. This can cut through the tendency to stay intellectual and rational, thus freeing the power of healing that comes from deep within and beyond the human individual experience.

For over two years, Mary has brought these poems to our therapeutic setting here at Recovery Plus. The words and emotions have touched patients and clients. They have been given permission to do their own sharing. The poems have been a part of their healing process.

These poems are a testament to personal and family healing. They bear witness to the healing that can happen when painful, traumatic and frightening emotions are expressed and let go. They give hope that families can bring about new levels of intimacy when secrets are brought to the light of day.

Now, through publication, these poems will be made available to a larger population who are participants in other treatment programs. I have no doubt that they can and will be a vital part of personal healing and growth.

FLIGHT ON NEW WINGS

I
Poems

FEBRUARY GIFT

1964

Beyond the hospital window, a muffled, white
    womb world. All night a blizzard storm
swirled, and now deep-drift curves glisten in blue
    morning sun like sparkled tissue paper
on a birthday gift. After labor's long night, you
    came forth from my womb's liquid dark,
transforming the season of cold and ice and tears,
    spring below the winter snow.

IN THE TENT
1970

We know you
> handsome smiling seminarian
> trusted friend of our friends
> minister of our church camping trip
> host of our child, invited to your tent

We do not know that you
> stalk our six-year-old son
> zip his sleeping bag to yours
> pull down his pajamas
> hurt his small body, his mind, his soul

We can never explain you
> who studies God
> who betrays this night
> who weaves a web to snare the young
> who scars our son for life

JAGGED PIECES

Black sky broke. A bolt
     of charged electric white cut
the night in jagged pieces.

A man stormed his darkness
     on the boy whose cry rose unheard.
Like lightning struck sky

wounds may meld back, but
     beneath this scar can one be wholly
healed, restored intact?

FALLOUT

the son

> *he picked me from all the kids*
> *he said he really liked me*
> *but he hurt me bad*
> *he lied to me*
>
> *i must be bad*
>
> *why didn't Daddy hit him, hurt him*
> *Mama and Daddy said he was sick*
> *but i didn't see him throw up*
> *they lied to me*
>
> *i must be bad*

the parents

> *betrayed by a Judas*
> *we walk in anger, sorrow, and shadow*
> *as though midday sun were eclipsed*
> *this pain is sharp against our days*
> *and at night tears mingle*

the therapist

> *I was on that camping trip*
> *I didn't tell you I had counseled him*
> *I thought he was cured*
> *I gambled and lost*

A MOTHER'S TRUTH

new worry turns round
my mind like a stone
lifted to light

fear
is my compass north

I know the stone's cold
concave, its inward weight
and sharp edge

I hide the fearstone
in daylight hours

but at night, carry it
to my soul's secret room
and hold it,

with my son,
in the curve of my heart

NIGHTMARE

in space
the seminarian crouches in a capsule
beyond time; above the curve of earth he
is alone, locked in the absolute absence of light

bitter cold
yet within him, shame burns hot
and raw-throated cries of guilt reverberate
within the void; a vortex of sorrow envelops his soul

on earth
prayers of those who loved him rise
on agitated wings, beat against the terrible
steel to release his soul, despairing in this prison

FIRST CONFESSION

eight years old

Sister says . . .
you will kneel
in a small dark space
you will whisper sins
you will be alone
with the priest

you bolt, fleeing
today's second grade
race home to your room
throw yourself on the bed
curve away from me
crying, with no words

we do not understand
your reaction
we do not make
the connection
we thought
you had forgotten

ANGER

in

late

July, sumac

lifts triangular

clusters of dense

blood - red seeds

impaling the air

like lance

tips

COMMON GROUND

ninth grade

He storms, slams out the kitchen door, pot
      and papers shoved in blue-plaid pocket.
He seeks a solitude: a place far from us,
      from rooms too small, demands too large.

A night fist fight in the park and he breaks
      a classmate's rib; he comes to table sullen,
skips school again, again the phone rings.
      Money is missing.   He asks for a kitten.

I wait in the car at the Humane Society
      and notice how brown winter grass begins
to tinge faint green. He returns carrying
      a coal black kitten and names him Mutzi.

At home, wrapped in the patchwork quilt
      I made for him, he cradles the purring Mutzi.
I am beside him. We stroke the kitten;
      for a brief moment   our hands touch.

DENIAL

I open the unlocked jewelry box
and remove an envelope
marked *Christmas*.

Heart races, hands shake.
I am hunter
and victim.

Suspicion consumes.
Cold coils into itself
with power to poison.

I count the bills;
darkness clouds my mind,
numbers jumble, tumble.

I count again, write it down,
do not believe, count again.
I plot against our son

and will watch, will stalk him.
Tomorrow when I count again,
I will know for sure.

Tomorrow comes,
clouds darken
to a deeper shade.

BEFORE MOTHER'S DAY

you are to mow
the overgrown lawn

you grumble, but begin
later you call from the backyard

looking out the kitchen window
I see

M O M

carved in the long sweet green

NEW LOVE

You turn from our love . . .
a yellow jacket in flight,

high on angry wings,
sipping purple thistles,

droning in nettle blooms,
clouds of angular dreams.

You mix the sweet, white
liquid, and a needle enters

your veins to rapture.
We are pierced.

AS YOU LEAVE, SHOUTS

slam the walls and my anger rises
    tall, needle-sharp like the pines
        that divide our own land.

For three days and nights
    December hoarfrost delicately
        feathers the evergreens.

Frost-thickened branches
    extend their splayed hands and
        offer fragile white peace.

You come home. We try again.

MOTHER AND SON

fear crouches
in my midnight room
and springs

I ride my terror . . .
a panther crashing
through frozen land
lost

while you ride
the white horse
powder in alley
rush

chaos
in our lives
like black ink
spilled on a winter
white blotter

WITH OR WITHOUT

Will it be like this for you,
with   or   without a fix;

will you be swept away
in OD rush
or in withdrawal?

Either way, a storm
will ravage your body.

DEATH UNDER THE INFLUENCE

the wake of our friend's son

his teammates come in sky-blue hockey jackets

stand silent as marble pillars and face his death

their captain's sun-tanned flesh now statue-cold

a scarlet-number jersey hides bloodless wounds

dark cheek bruises rise under layers of disguise

eyelight gone, auburn hair splayed against satin

dead fingers curve to touch favorite fishing lures

teammates look away,   sink in a sea of sorrow

DREAM OF DEATH

Our son stands,
a bas-relief carved
dark upon the hill.

He turns utterly
away from me
and step by step

descends into
churning water,
unable to swim.

My hands reach
out; blind fingers
press emptiness.

WHIRLING THE VORTEX
Sunday's offering, stolen

We find him in the family room.
Why did you?   Anger leaps
like flames from father and son.

Granite fear freezes me;
understanding them
I know how this will end.

Son's eyes rage;
he rushes up the stairs,
slams out the door, is gone.

Fire flares in his father's hands.
Fists rise,
clenching.

Whirling the vortex
I lose my
self and cry, *hit me*,

but his fists seek and strike
the couch,
again and again.

Storm splinters our home
from inside out;   together
we are driven apart,   fiercely.

WHO ARE YOU?

In this web,
>   spun from the landscape of addiction,
>   spider and fly eye each other.

Fly is frantic,
>   caught in tensile web threads. He struggles,
>   buzzes his wings, a prisoner.

Spider craves,
>   hungers to consume his prey. Deft legs weave
>   spinneret filaments,

And fly dies
>   within gray-shrouded walls, a hoarded stash
>   to feed spider's coming need.

Are you spider
>   living in the landscape you formed, waiting
>   to devour?

Are you fly
>   waiting to be devoured?

THE CHOICE
husband or son

i am soul spent
hands twist red

in deadlock
i face myself

divided, as though
two beasts, tightly

leashed, struggle
for release and

breaking free
attack

CRISIS

i am weak with lack.
it is wide and deep
as the Pacific
and sweeps over
my days and nights
in endless waves.

feckless as foam
i am hurled
here, there,
cast ashore
in unknown land.
like a brown shell,
beached and drained
upon the sand,
i am mottled white
with fear.
i gulp cold spray
as the ocean drowns
my small voice down.

salt of shame,
sorrow and anger
tastes bitter
on my parched tongue.
eyes burn shut,
my mouth,   mute.

BREAK POINT

point:
  a crucial situation in a course of events

                              yes

break:
  to fracture without separate pieces
  to swerve from a straight path
  to pierce, to intrude upon, to crack
  to overwhelm with grief

                                  yes

IN DARKEST HOURS

i enter a galaxy of poetry, and like stars
poems flicker ageless
truth across my night. i whisper words
familiar as daily prayers
that slip through my mind, line by line,
move like beads in my
fingers and give comfort, like the truth
my parents are present
still, interceding for me, for our family,
like the truth of dawning
sun, the silence of mottled moon. stars,
sun, moon, and earth turn me,
this room, this night and curve to listen.
i tell my one small life.

APRIL COMES COLD

on north wind breath, yet finches return early

to flutter the highest maple limbs, unraveling

red-throated song like spooled ribbon flung

across the dawn, yet I am as fallow ground,

frozen, our son lost in a storm of addiction.

Turning homeward, I journey back, yearning

to see the wet, black fields of winter wheat

coming green.

My mother opens the farmhouse door, singing.

WEAVING THE WHITE LINE

police

                        car at the curb

and

we

                        caught in

the mid-
night whirl

                        the revolving light

you scream
    you hate us
      you

cry

                        say you will never
                        forgive

at the A & C unit

for

                        your seventeenth
                                  birthday

we fill
out forms

                        we commit you

for evaluation

                        across the room
                              we watch

you

a prisoner

                        caught
                        in this circle
                              of chairs

clad in hospital
pajamas

you
turn . . .

                        and say,
                        hi, I'm . . .
                        alcoholic
                        addict

DETOX

cries and moans exit
the almost closed door,
find my ears and enter

hospital personnel rush
muffled pleas for quiet

your gorge rises; terror
and curses splinter the air

the door slams shut; still
sounds etch the marrow
of my bones, burn like acid

HARD ROAD

he does not want this pain
that begs him
turn
from gut-cold cramps, shaking, body sweats

He does not want this pain
that begs Him
turn
from anguish, dragging the cross of Calvary

FROM THE DEPTHS
guilt and grace

Gnarled guilt twists my soul
like a wounded bird in flight.
I hear righteous voices clamor
in a chorus of dissonant song,
harping sharp on north wind,
my own voice, loudest of all.

Sorrow and I flail against air,
wings heavy and pain-weary;
deep is my wound, yet I hear
an inner voice whisper, come,
settle softly here. Rest easy

in circled olive branches, rest
easy in the depth of your soul.
Be embraced. You will learn
to sing compassion, like mist,
to sing forgiveness, like dew,
to sing peace, like spring rain.

DESIGN

Outside the hospital window
     a spider's web is hung, spun
          against the dazzle of sun.

The web is flawed, its pattern
     imperfect, yet perfect drops
          of morning dew cling

to tensile threads like tears
     and refract eastern sunlight
          within each pristine drop.

Prism colors shimmer, shine.
     Web and sun and dew
          evolve a new design.

WILLOWS IN BABYLON SPRING

By the waters of Babylon, there we sat down
and wept when we remembered Zion.
On the willows there we hung our harps.
Psalm 137

By waters of the Mississippi, sorrow flows
from arched weeping willows. Thin spine
tendrils bend low, bring forth spring leaves,
myriad tapered tears from a fountain of grief.

No longer does music pleasure my soul; no
longer do guitar hands strum taut strings; no
longer does lyric song open clenched throat.
You are exiled from home and me and family,

yet love remains, deep as the memory of music.

ACKNOWLEDGMENT

Black crows
croak their
raucous din

in curious
sets of three
and riddle thin

the air's sacred
silence
again and again.

I have tried, but
can not forgive
the man.   When

I imagine our son,
the dark tent
and him . . .

my wound opens;
hate gnaws
my soul thin.

Must I forgive
for healing
to begin?

NEW DREAMS

Here, in this place, old desires glitter like
                    crystal snow and ice,
entice your body and soul to ride again
                      the rush of avalanche.
Yet you long for days patterned with truth,
                    peace,   hope,   joy.

Here, in this place, circled by friends and
                    wedded to a will of fire,
old desires melt, anoint parched ground
                    to water thirsting roots.
New leaves will brush the sky; new dreams,
                  like young birds,   fly.

FIRST WEEKEND PASS

Hope knocks on the door
and enters.

Outside, loud music rocks
as you wash your Chevy Impala,
throw old clutter in the trash.
Your father, me, you,
nervous as new love
during supper.

But your will of steel rams
against the law,
against us.
You drive off
without a license.
How dare you!

I hear your father, sick
again, and I breathe
again the air of despair.
My mind spins a mantra:
let go, let God;
let go, let God . . .

You return.
Supper dishes still undone.
Silence smolders like old fire
in every room;
ashes drift the dark
as we drive you back.

I type the letter, words
wound the page:
. . . cannot come home
. . . a halfway house
. . . your father and I
   cannot live like this.

Hope opens the door
and leaves.

THE SHADOW SELF

Tonight,
I discover myself
divided; two mirror images reflect

and move in the double-paned window;
each knows the other is an imposter

and both are suspicious of me.

My fingertips probe
the marrow of my blind soul, read

its raised Braille shadow and see;
the imposter lives
here,   in me.

RELEASED

After a hard frost,
dominant, green-leaf color fades
and autumn's dormant hues
rise, emerge,
painting a palette of rich colors.

After addiction
submerges you in dark,
monochrome days, you turn,
rise, emerge
to a world of color, released.

WHAT LILA SAID

in group

There's a hole in my soul, she said.
It cannot be filled with drugs, sex,
gambling, power, or another person.

The hole in my soul is like a dormant
volcano circled by walls of rock

but blame, shame, anger erupt like lava,
spill molten chaos across my life.

May the hole in my soul be filled
by my higher power who enters, calms

and joins me to heal old wounds
as I choose to walk new steps.

There is a hole in my soul, yet here
I will come to know myself,
know my power to become whole.

TOWARD FLIGHT

Spring Azure butterfly

Our son, long confined in his prison of addiction,
aches to be set free. He, like a chrysalis,
feels walls encasing him . . . walls
formed by his other self, his other life.

You emerge, Spring Azure.   Iridescent
wings unfold . . . dry . . . flex against
unknown air, pulse with first breath
in the stunning light of rebirth.

Our son trembles on the edge,
pauses . . . chooses . . . opens. Released
from crumbling walls of darkness,
he breathes the clear light of morning.

Rising above the sunned green of spring,
flight on new wings.

HAIKU

emerge from darkness
    embrace the light of new truth
white lilies blossom

ORATORIO

In our greening front yard
April's first forsythia
bursts from slender branch
tombs like a fountain
cascading small four-petal
blooms of yellow sun,
spilled
alleluia!

NOTHING BUT BLUE SKIES

they meet at AA
honey-blonde she
full of ginger spice
husky laugh

rugged-handsome he
good times shaker
black leather jacket
motorcycle roar

they cling   Harley-
ride the highway
as voices sing hard
against the wind

hope soars untamed
a flash of cardinal
song against Blue
Ridge Mountain air

on a sunflower day
two vows   to love
forever   to stay
straight

CRASH AT TYSON'S CORNER

braked tires squeal
a car impacts your cycle
and loose helmet arcs the air
you land on your head

       you fight ambulance medics
       are strapped in restraints
       air-lifted to D.C. trauma center
       stung with hypos for pain
       cannot name pregnant wife
       cannot name pencil, apple, cup
       cannot read
       cannot work for six months
       cannot drive a car for a year

you, recovering from addiction
are struck by a drunk teen-driver
who walks away unhurt, while
you begin another journey

THAT NIGHT

After you find your wife and her lover
drunk, naked, in your bed
and your small son in the next room,
a fist of rage smashes into the windshield's
shatterless glass, spreading a web
of jagged lines driven
from the center.

In dawn light you touch the windshield
held in place like a fractured still life;
your fingers trace the edge
of blood.

REMAINS

Winched up
on back wheels by a wrecking truck,
the white Prizm is collapsed like a metal accordion,
every window frame emptied of glass.
Two green **X**'s scrawled by clean-up crew on
crumpled trunk and angled roof mean
"parts only" for salvage. Shatterproof windshield lies
draped like a patterned tablecloth
over dashboard and steering wheel in eerie beauty;
shards of glass held in place
like skin cells under a microscope.
Any life to salvage?

DIVORCE

Your small son cries, *Mama*, in the night.

> You hurl a family photo
> in the trash; wedding
> ring lies in an ashtray.

Your small son cries, *Mama.*

> Your days are etched
> with acid anger; raw
> wounds do not heal.

Your small son cries.

> With no mama near
> long hours are tears
> on a winter shroud.

Your small son.

> A green thirst rises
> in you; spring growth
> waits, unseen.

Your son.

MY SON

When others speak of your circular sorrow,
      soul grim, washed with Gethsemane tears
and flesh gone thin across angular bones,
      I turn on the wheel of your pain, but always
that certain distance apart. My hands reach
      out to slow your reeling center and the pulse
of my heart listens to your jagged silence,
      the weal-edge of broken words. As the thread
of your life unspools, I am entwined, drawn
                          into your wound.

WILLOW, GREEN WILLOW

His family divided
like a stand of willows,
chainsaw cut.

The back porch he began
years ago, unfinished:
ceiling riven with twisted
nails, bare slanting studs,
wiring visible,
but outside
walls are smooth with siding,
a facade to neighbors
of a porch completed,
a family united.

This August
he drives back, alone.
For nine days he builds
himself: by measure,
by saw, by hammer,
by plaster, by panel.
We watch.

Small green shoots
begin to rise from roots
of severed willows.

FAMILY

It is not the sunlit, leaded prism
    with refracted, blended colors
        splashing the wall that engages me.

No, it is the twelve-point, glass star
    that casts uncolored patterns: ovals,
        oblongs and orbs.   As air warms, rises,

light shapes move back and forth, up
    and down in sun dance, like a gathering
        of family. Some designs are fractured

by shadow lines, others remain whole
    in this galaxy of motion, pulsing strong,
        drawing close to wounded others, like healers.

Clustered daystars return again and
    again to their Source, ride the breath
        of sun, transcending my March morning.

BLUEPRINT

twenty-two years straight

you

       open the door to your higher power
       are granted full custody of your son
       walk the day-by-day path of AA

you

       rebuild the inner rooms of your home
       become a carpenter of excellent craft
       form your own construction company

you

       remodel old into new

THE POTTER, THE CLAY

we are the clay and You the potter
Isaiah 64:7

He spins a bit of earth, the earth spins him.

Treadle wheel circles and turntable hums

as he bends his breath of creation above

a mound of ruddy clay to shape inner space,

to achieve a design. The same pot does not

happen twice. Earthen vessels are formed,

glazed, fired and filled, brought to final beauty;

we wait.

I DO NOT WANT TO SING MY DANCING SHOES TO SLEEP

Dance, then, wherever you may be.
I am the Lord of the dance, said he.
                                    Shaker Song

I want to lift my soul while dawn
                    unfurls, pale as periwinkle ribbon

I want to walk full stride, unlimping
                    and mark a path in morning dew

I want to seek counsel for a daughter's
                    thoughtful, troubling questions

I want to bring tea roses to my face,
                    feast on their June-yellow perfume

I want to touch my husband's white hair,
                    brush his lined face with my lips

I want to taste the spicy pumpkin pie
                    cooling in the kitchen for supper

I want to look into our son's clear eyes,
                    thankful for sober, carpenter hands

I want to peel away the layers of days,
                    memorize moments of small beauty

I want to gather and hold the all of my life,
                    this joy, that sorrow, but most of all,

I do not want to sing my dancing shoes
                    to sleep . . . no, no . . . not now.

FLIGHT ON NEW WINGS

II
Addendum

What Is Poetry Therapy?

"Poetry therapy is the intentional use of the written and spoken word for healing and personal growth."

—The Integrative Medicine Committee,
The National Association for Poetry Therapy

A Basic Premise of Poetry Therapy

When employing poetry therapy as a mode of healing and personal growth, it is the interaction between the individual, the trained facilitator and the poem that make up the three components inherent to the dynamics of poetry therapy. The poem becomes the meeting ground where emotional response and dialogue occur, opening the possibility of new personal insights leading to greater self-knowledge.

Objectives for Using Poetry in Therapy

—to become aware of one's thoughts and feelings through response to literature
—to clarify and define oneself by stating one's thoughts and feelings
—to come to terms with one's explosive or elusive emotions
—to bring order and clarity to chaotic thoughts and feelings
—to use writing as a means of expression and sharing
—to interact with others in a group, respecting their reactions and statements
—to enhance a sense of belonging
—to stimulate the senses, creative imagination and recollection

Used with permission. Original title: "Objectives for Using Literature In
Therapy." Heller, P. O., Ph.D., The Wordsworth Center. 1998.

Arleen McCarty Hynes and Mary Hynes-Berry have written an excellent and comprehensive textbook in which the major goals and objectives of biblio/poetry therapy are defined in great detail. (See *Biblio/Poetry Therapy, An Interactive Handbook*, North Star Press of St. Cloud, Inc., 1994, pp. 77-78.)

For Whom Is Poetry Therapy Intended?

The poems in *Flight on New Wings* are currently used in the clinical setting of a hospital and relate to sexual abuse, addiction, and recovery. Appropriate poems can be used for any one person undergoing therapy or for groups that have as their goal healing and personal growth, whether in a clinical setting or not. Some examples of people who have found poetry therapy beneficial for healing are those who have experienced divorce or depression; those who have suffered the loss of a loved one; those who are ill in hospitals, hospice care, or nursing homes and those in prisons and mental institutions.

Others who may have personal growth as their primary goal might be young or older married couples, new parents, adolescents, college students, those wishing to improve parent-child relationships or those belonging to a religious order.

It is important that the therapist carefully choose appropriate poems, whether for healing or for personal growth, that relate to the particular life situations, feeling states, and goals of the individuals with whom they are working.

WHY USE POETRY AS THERAPY?

Poetry can play a very special part in the psychotherapeutic process.

> First: Poems tend to be short.
> Second: They are often constructed so as to appeal to the emotions and senses.
> Third: They can aim for a central point like an arrow to a bull's eye.
>> An adaptation from the "Foreword" by Raymond J. Corsini, Ph.D., from *Poetry in the Therapeutic Experience*, edited by Arthur Lerner, Ph.D., R.P.T., MMB Music, Inc. 1978, 1994, p. ix.

First: Poem Length

A brief poem has an advantage over long poems and prose pieces because the subject matter is more focused and concisely conveyed thus allowing the opportunity for a personal response almost immediately. Most people can remain more attentive when short pieces are used. This is especially true of those who are in the early stages of treatment and who may be experiencing withdrawal symptoms and/or the inability to concentrate. During a ninety-minute group session two or three poems, which give a variety of perspectives inherent to addiction and recovery, may be processed. (In an on-going poetry therapy program however, where the same people return for several meetings, one poem and a writing exercise may be sufficient for each session.) The size of the group and time constraints may also militate against using long poems or prose works.

Second: Emotional Impact

Poems have the power to go directly to the heart, emotions, and senses as well as to the mind and spirit. Often the troubled feelings and emotions of an addicted person have been dulled through the use of drugs and alcohol. Part of the work of poetry therapy in a clinical setting for addiction is to surface the painful feelings and emotions of the addicted person. Appropriate poems, presented by the therapist, can be helpful in guiding those in treatment to face their troubled lives in a safe, drug-free and educational environment. Using poems for "family groups" or "after care" or "relapse" groups can also surface deep, unresolved feelings and be beneficial to participants. In the format of a poetry therapy session it is imperative that there be a progression from describing a difficult situation to a concluding discussion or a final poem that offers as its central point a positive, hopeful view of the person's recovery from addiction.

Third: Poem Focus

Poems often contain a kernel of truth, a central point, or a universality that may allow the listener or reader to identify with the situation and the emotions portrayed in the poem. Participants will realize they are not alone in their problems. The poem can bring personal validation and act as a voice that echoes their own feelings and experience.

There is also an advantage to a poem that has ambiguous words or meaning. This allows for an individual's personal reading and for the juxtaposition of varied perspectives or reactions to the same words or phrases from different members of a group.

AN OVERVIEW OF A POETRY THERAPY SESSION

A poem is read aloud as participants follow with their own copies. It is well to read the poem aloud a second time, either by a volunteer or by the group. The well known poet, Robert Bly, has said that when reading or listening to a poem the first time, we hear it with the "ear of the mind" and the second time, we hear it with the "ear of the heart."

Participants silently examine the emotions, images, sensations, and thoughts they experienced as the poem was read and write them down.

Participants are given the opportunity to share their written responses orally, or if they choose not to speak they may say, "pass." All listen respectfully to the responses and comments of others. Many times these responses begin a dialogue within the group.

Participants are directed to circle words, phrases, or lines of the distributed poem that relate to their own lives. They may choose to share the circled words and the reasons why the words are significant, either orally or in writing. In the Addendum, each poem has companion questions that also may act as the basis of a discussion or a written response.

Through discussion, guided by the facilitator/therapist, new insights and reactions are shared by the group.

ADDITIONAL CONSIDERATIONS

One of the facilitator's major roles is to listen attentively to the patients' words and carefully observe their non-verbal communication, which may give clues about their feelings. The facilitator can offer, at opportune moments, pertinent, gentle interjections such as: can you tell us a little more about that, or, I can see you have strong feelings about this. Using open-ended questions that begin with words such as: when, how, where, or what were your feelings then, or now, may help to bring new insights to the patient.

Sometimes, because of the personal, sensitive nature of a subject or experience, it may be wise to suggest that a written response be made. This activity may allow for more openness than the usual format of speaking in front of the group. When individuals write a response or create their own poem, unresolved feelings often surface and self-awareness often increases.

Each response to a poem is regarded by the therapist and others in the group as being valid and true, whether spoken or written. This affirmation helps to establish a level of trust among participants.

The sessions are not an English class where a poem is analyzed, nor is it important that written responses be grammatically correct. Rather, it is an opportunity to react on a feeling level to the poem's words, phrases, or subject matter which may relate to one's own life.

During the process of working through a poem, the therapist should be aware that participants may develop a new attitude about their own life in the past, the present or for the future. They should be encouraged to share their new awareness with the group. Sometimes a fleeting concept that the patient has thought about in the past may crystallize because of a new perception or insight into the subject matter of the poem.

It is important that the rules of confidentiality are understood from the beginning of the poetry-therapy experience and are maintained after the session ends.

The poems in *Flight on New Wings* follow a linear sequence, but do not have to be presented or processed in consecutive order.

WHO ARE CERTIFIED POETRY THERAPISTS (CPT) OR REGISTERED POETRY THERAPISTS (RPT)

Thousands of counselors and therapists use poetry and other forms of literature to foster personal growth and help achieve therapeutic goals with clients, but . . .

the only persons authorized to call themselves poetry therapists are those who have fulfilled the training requirements and who have been awarded or who are eligible to be awarded the designation of either certified poetry therapist (CPT) or registered poetry therapist (RPT) by the certification committee of the National Federation for Biblio/Poetry Therapy.

For more information, contact **www.poetrytherapy.org** and click on "Training and Education."

FORMAT FOR A POETRY THERAPY SESSION IN A RECOVERY PROGRAM

I. The participants fill out name tags as they enter (first name only) and sit in a circle. Later their attention will be directed to the following statements and questions written on the board:

      a. The definition of poetry therapy.
      b. What do you think this poem is about?
      c. How does the poem make you feel?
      d. Circle words or phrases in the poem that relate to your life.

II. Introductions are given.
The facilitator or therapist gives a brief description of poetry therapy as another "tool" of recovery and the format of the session.
(Small groups of 5-12 participants are preferred rather than larger groups of 13-25.)

III. Show or hand out an example of realia (picture or art object) that will be a partner to the poem being "processed." Realia can be used as an ice-breaker or a lead-in to a poem and should be related to the poem in some way. Many poems will not need to have accompanying pictures or art objects, but often they enhance the meaning and sensory appeal of a poem in a significant way.

IV. Hand out copies of one poem. Participants follow along as the poem is read aloud. It may be read aloud a second time by a volunteer or together, as a group.

V. Participants are asked to answer question (b.) orally. Next they write in response to question (c.) their own "feeling words" . . . (angry, sad, joyful, hopeful, etc.) The "feeling words" they experienced through the poem's text are shared and discussed.

VI. Participants are invited to circle words or phrases (d.) relating to their own lives. All are encouraged to share their circled words, but they may choose to be silent and say "pass." The facilitator may ask some people why a circled word was significant or which word was most significant and why. Additional discussion may occur when a poem's companion questions in the Addendum are utilized by the therapist or when the companion questions become the basis for an individual's written response which can be shared with the group. (Each poem in the Addendum is numbered by the page on which it occurs.)

VII.   Participants could also be asked to write a poem or paragraph after the session ends using some of their circled words or phrases about the subject of their addiction or recovery process. Completed poems or paragraphs could be shared later with their primary group or given to their counselors.

VIII.   At the end of processing a poem, there may be a discussion about the relevance of the realia in light of the poem's subject matter, or addiction, or their recovery program.

IX.   Process one or two more poems as time allows, following the same format. Close with an up-beat, hopeful poem or a discussion that gives positive affirmation for recovery.

X.   Finally, the facilitator asks for any additional reactions, new insights, or comments from the group as a whole. If poems are used in a multi-session program, where the same participants return for a specified number of weeks, a reading or writing assignment for the next session may be given. If desired, session evaluations can be filled out and handed in, to be read by the staff. Close with the Serenity Prayer.

These questions, directed to the persons in treatment or to their parents, are only a place to begin a discussion or a written reaction. Questions that are designated for "parents" may be adapted for family members or others who are significant in the patient's life. Counselors and therapists are encouraged to assess and adapt the suggested questions for other addictions as well as to develop their own questions from their knowledge and understanding of a particular group. There may be other issues raised by the poems and they should be addressed appropriately.

Beneath the title of most poems a suggested realia is listed which can be used as a lead-in to the poem, a final thought about the poem, or both. Most often the realia used in Recovery Plus poetry therapy sessions have been pictures, but objects related to the poems have also been used. Therapists are always free to develop their own realia rather than the one suggested or to use the poem without an accompanying realia. The number before the poem refers to the page on which it is found.

3. "February Gift"
> Suggested Realia: a picture of spring flowers blooming in the snow.

What emotions might the coming of a new baby evoke in parents?

What hopes or dreams might your parents have had for you?

When you become a parent, what hopes or dreams might you have for your child?

Parents: What hopes or dreams did you have for your child, who is in treatment, before he/she was born? What are your hopes and dreams for your child now?

4. "In the Tent"
> Suggested Realia: a picture of a tent and campground.

If something like this happened to you as a child, or another kind of abuse, what did you do?

What difference has that experience made in your life?

Can you write about that experience and your feelings at that time?

5. "Jagged Pieces"

Suggested Realia: a picture of lightning against a dark sky.

Have you ever wondered if a person can recover completely from a traumatic experience such as abuse? What are your thoughts?

What are the hindrances to recovery?

What would help an abused person recover?

6. "Fallout"

What are your feelings about the person who betrayed you?

Did you have anybody you could talk to about the event right after it occurred?

Do you have anybody to talk to now?

If another kind of abuse/trauma has happened to you, write about it.

Parents: What are your feelings now about the person who betrayed your child?

7. "A Mother's Truth"

Suggested Realia: small granite chips or rocks for each person to hold and describe.

Parents: What feelings might you have if an abusive experience had happened to your child?

In what way do you identify with the mother's worry and fear in the poem?

What actions could you take after discovering your child has been abused?

8. "Nightmare"

When have you felt isolated and filled with guilt, sorrow, despair?

What, for you, is a path out of these emotions?

9. "First Confession"

> *Parents: Do you remember any behavior of your child who is in treatment that may have been a clue that he or she had a very negative experience? If so, what was the behavior?*
>
> *How did you react to your child's behavior?*

10. "Anger"

Suggested Realia: an actual sumac seed-cluster or a picture of one.

What makes you most angry?

What images best capture your anger? What does it look like, sound like, feel like?

What has anger or fear driven you to do?

What new ways have you learned to manage anger?

11. "Common Ground"

Suggested Realia: picture of an all black cat.

What does your pet offer to you? What do you offer to your pet?

Write a letter (that may or may not be sent) thanking a person for their unconditional love.

> *Parents: What emotions have you felt because of your child's behavior? How can those emotions be dealt with to achieve a positive outcome?*

12. "Denial"

Suggested Realia: an empty jewelry box.

When did denial happen in your home, in your loved ones, or in yourself?

What purpose did denial serve?

What are the negative effects of denial?

13. "Before Mother's Day"
Suggested Realia: a picture of a lawn mower.

Suggest some ways you can show affection when things aren't going well between you and your loved ones.

In what ways does it help to show love?

In what ways have others shown their love to you?

14. "New Love"

What thoughts or feelings might your parents and siblings have had concerning your drug or alcohol use?

Compare "falling in love" with a person to "falling in love" with drugs or alcohol.

Parents: What did you think and feel about your child when you knew he or she was abusing alcohol or drugs?

15. "As You Leave, Shouts"
Suggested Realia: a picture of frost or snow-laden evergreen branches.

What is your reaction to this poem?

What did you do when anger, like a volcano, built up and exploded?

What did others around you do when your anger exploded?

16. "Mother and Son"
Suggested Realia: a black ink blot on white paper.

Write about a specific time in your life when chaos engulfed you.

Have you ever thought what your parents might have worried about when you were out for the night? What would it be like to be in their shoes?

Parents: In what ways does this poem speak to you?

17. "With or Without"

What is your reaction to this poem?

What might help you during this time of withdrawal?

Describe how you felt when you were unable to take your drug of choice.

18. "Death Under the Influence"
Suggested Realia: a hockey jersey or picture of an open casket and flowers.

Have you attended the wake or funeral of a friend who died under the influence of drugs or alcohol? Write about your thoughts at that time.

What are your feelings about your own death?

Might it happen as a result of drugs and alcohol?

What positive qualities might people remember about you at your wake or funeral?

19. "Dream of Death"

What frightening dreams have you had about yourself?

Is there a recurring dream? If so, write what you remember about it.

Parents: What dreams about your child have frightened you?

20. "Whirling the Vortex"
Suggested Realia: a picture of a dark tornado funnel.

Has anything similar happened in your family? Can you tell us or write about it?

What emotions and additional problems might swirl around addiction?

Give examples of co-dependent behavior that you have observed in others.

Parents: How have you experienced co-dependency in yourself?

21. "Who Are You"

Suggested Realia: a picture of a spider, web, and caught fly.

Before coming to treatment were you like the spider or the fly in the poem?

What does the phrase "landscape of addiction" mean to you?

After treatment what specific actions will you take to spin a new "landscape"?

22. "The Choice"

Describe a time when you felt "torn in two" or when you faced an agonizing choice.

What sources of support are there for you now when you feel torn between addiction and sobriety?

Parents: When did you feel you had to make a choice between your child and your spouse?

23. "Crisis"

Suggested Realia: a picture of ocean waves in a storm.

When have you felt overwhelmed by a situation? Write about that time.

What helped you cope with your feelings?

Parents: When have you felt a time of crisis? Write about that time.

24. "Break Point"

What feelings does this poem express that relate to your situation?

What images does the term "break point" evoke for you?

25. "In Darkest Hours"

Suggested Realia: a picture of stars against a dark sky.

Before coming to treatment how did you escape in times of trouble?

Name some healthy ways to deal with the dark hours of trouble.

Parents: Where did you find help or relief from your worries about your child?

26. "April Comes Cold"

In the past, with whom did you find peace and acceptance in a drug free environment? Write a letter (that may or may not be sent) thanking that person.

Describe a favorite place of peace where you like to go now. Relish that peace again.

Parents: Where might you find peace in a time of crisis?

27. "Weaving the White Line"

Suggested Realia: the shape of the poem on the page forms the realia.

What happened that brought you into treatment?

What fears and assumptions did you have about treatment?

Write your own poem beginning with a line or phrase from this poem.

Parents: What were your feelings about your child coming to treatment?

28. "Detox"

When have you witnessed or experienced someone going through detox? (TV, movies, books, real life?)

What impact did it have on you?

Compare and contrast what you saw on TV or in movies to your own experience of withdrawing from drugs or alcohol.

29. "Hard Road"

What are your thoughts about physical and mental suffering brought about by addiction?

What part does suffering play in your recovery?

How can your Higher Power help smooth the road to recovery?

30. "From the Depths"

Suggested Realia: a picture of a beautiful green tree.

What does "guilt" look like? Draw a picture of your symbol for guilt or describe it in words.

Why is forgiving yourself so difficult? Why is it important?

What symbolizes "peace" for you? Draw a picture of it or describe it in words.

Which of the Twelve Steps will bring you the greatest sense of peace?

31. "Design"

> Suggested Realia: a picture of a spider web with clinging dew drops.

Though the spider's web is flawed, in dewed sunlight it is still beautiful. What connection might these words have to you?

What flaws and strengths in yourself and others do you tend to notice?

What is your design for a new life?

32. "Willows in Babylon Spring"

> Suggested Realia: picture of a person playing a guitar.

What feelings do you think your loved ones are experiencing in your absence: sorrow, relief, anger, hope? Write your thoughts about their feelings.

Write a letter to a loved one (that may or may not be sent) expressing your feelings about your absence from them.

Parents: How does the poem reflect your feelings about your child's absence from home?

33. "Acknowledgment"

Which of the Twelve Steps does this poem lead us to examine?

The poem asks: Is forgiveness part of the healing process? What are your thoughts about forgiveness in your life?

34. "New Dreams"

> Suggested Realia: a picture of birds in flight or a single bird, perhaps a dove.

How do you cope with the old feelings of craving when they occur?

What does "a will of fire" mean to you?

Has a "will of fire" been more of a negative or a positive response in your life? What has it lead you to do? Write about this.

35. "First Weekend Pass"

What is a symbol of hope for you? Draw it or describe it in words.

Compare your first weekend pass or time away from treatment to the one described in the poem.

When have you experienced a "will of steel" in making choices?

Parents: What "mantra" do you or can you say in times of trouble?

36. "The Shadow Self"

Suggested Realia: a picture of someone looking into a mirror.

The poem speaks about an imposter living inside us. When have you experienced this?

What does your imposter look like, say, or do?

How is the imposter part of denial? What steps can you take to free yourself from the imposter within?

37. "Released"

Suggested Realia: a picture showing a variety of colored autumn leaves.

What word(s) would you use to describe your life on drugs?

In what ways has your life become a "monochrome" since becoming involved in a life of drugs?

What specific actions can you take to bring natural "color" back into your daily life?

38. "What Lila Said"

Suggested Realia: a picture of a volcano crater and/or one that is erupting.

How have you tried to fill the hole in your soul?

Write about an incident when you formed walls around yourself.

What part has shame, blame and anger played in your choosing to use drugs?

Name specific ways in which treatment can help you grow "healthy and whole."

39. "Toward Flight"

Suggested Realia: the picture on the cover of *Flight on New Wings*.

What is the hardest part of your struggle toward sobriety?

How can you begin to prepare now to meet the challenges after treatment?

Write a description about your time of spiritual awakening.

40. "Haiku"

Suggested Realia: a picture of Easter lilies.

What do you think "white lilies" symbolize?

Write your own seventeen-syllable haiku or short poem, using three words from this poem or three words that describe yourself right now.

41. "Oratorio"

Suggested Realia: a picture of a forsythia bush in bloom.

Parents: What were your feelings when your child went into treatment?

How might Parents Anonymous or Al-Anon help you?

42. "Nothing but Blue Skies"

Suggested Realia: a picture of a motorcycle.

What leads a person to vow to "stay straight"?

Is making a vow for a loved one's sake sufficient reason to "stay straight"?

What causes people to break their vow?

43. "Crash at Tyson's Corner"

Suggested Realia: a picture of an ambulance.

After treatment, what might you do to keep your sobriety if adversity occurs?

If you experience a "slip," what will give you courage to begin again?

44. "That Night"

Suggested Realia: a picture of a smashed car windshield.

What events have fractured your life?

What have the consequences been to you?

What have the consequences been to your loved ones?

45. "Remains"

Suggested Realia: a poster of James Dean's crashed car.

Was there a time when parts of your life felt totaled, like the car in the poem? Describe that time, using any images that fit for you.

What helped you move on?

46. "Divorce"

Suggested Realia: a picture of a parent and young child having fun together.

How can a person maintain recovery after divorce?

If you are divorced, what point of view was most helpful for you during the process?

47. "My Son"

Parents: What is the meaning of the line, "I turn on the wheel of your pain"?

When have you felt drawn into a loved one's pain?

What advice would you give this parent?

48. "Willow, Green Willow"

How can you bring healing to the broken relationships in your life? Be specific.

Which of the Twelve Steps does this poem reflect?

What new "sense of self" has treatment released for you here, in the hospital?

How can you continue your growth as a person after you leave the hospital?

What can you see yourself "building"?

49. "Family"

Suggested Realia: a crystal prism or a glass star.

Does your personality seem more like the sunlit prism's showy rainbow or more like an uncolored light reflection? Explain your answer.

Recall a specific time in your life when you felt fractured. Write about that time.

Who in your family, or in your circle of friends, has been a healer for you? Describe an incident when that person tried to help you. Write a letter of gratitude to that person.

The poem uses the phrase "return again and again to their Source." What does that mean to you?

50. "Blueprint"

Suggested Realia: an actual blueprint.

How do you see your life after treatment? A year from now?

What is your blueprint for the future?

What place does your Higher Power have in your life's plan?

51. "The Potter, the Clay"

Suggested Realia: a piece of pottery, a bowl or vase.

What gifts do you possess that make you unique?

Describe yourself as a specific clay figure "brought to final beauty." What design, shape, glaze, purpose do you envision?

Have past events led you to believe your Higher Power has a plan for your life of recovery?

Can you write about a specific time when you felt your life was spared?

How will your Higher Power influence the way you live after treatment?

52. "I Do Not Want to Sing My Dancing Shoes to Sleep"

The poem speaks about holding the "all of life . . . joys and sorrows." Why is it important to remember sorrows as well as joys?

What lessons have your sorrows taught you?

What lessons have your joys taught you?

Write a list of things you want to do in your life after graduation from treatment.

Parents: Make a list of enjoyable experiences you might like to have with your loved one after treatment is completed.

RESPONSE TO THE POETRY SESSION

Your First Name: (optional)_____Date_____

POEM TITLES:__

1._____2._____3._____

1. How was this session meaningful for you?

2. What feelings or new insights did you gain about your <u>past</u> addiction?

3. What new insights did you gain about your <u>future</u> road to recovery?

4. Might you read the poems again and think about their relation to your life? Yes/No
      Please explain your answer.

5. Your overall reaction to the poetry therapy session was:

Additional comments or suggestions?

Credits

The following poems were originally published in *Quilt Pieces*:
"February Gift," "Common Ground," "Mother and Son," "April Comes Cold," and "Toward Flight."

Grants and Awards

Received an Honorable Mention cash award from the Central Minnesota Arts Board grant competition, 2002.

Received a $2000 Individual Artist In Poetry grant from the Central Minnesota Arts Board, 1998.

Awarded First Place for the poem, "Gettysburg," history category, Mississippi Valley Poetry Contest, 1992; Twelfth Place in the *Writer's Digest* contest, 1994.

Additional Publications

Poems have appeared in the following literary magazines, anthologies and newspapers:

Minnesota Calendar of Poetry (3 years), *Studio One, Black Hat Press, Loonfeather, North Coast Review, Lower Stumpf Lake Review, Nostalgia, Anthology of Space and Sky, Diotima, Native West Press, Sisters Today, The Moccasin, Divine Favor: The Art of Joseph O'Connell*, Liturgical Press, *National Catholic Reporter, The St. Cloud Visitor,* and *Muse.*

About the Author

Born on a southern Minnesota farm, Mary Willette Hughes was the only daughter in a family of six children. She attended a one-room schoolhouse for eight years, the local high school in Delavan and then earned a Bachelors Degree in Music at the College of St. Benedict. For the next sixteen years, she was a full-time wife and mother, parenting seven children with her husband, Mark. She spent several years as a grade school music teacher, overlapping with years as a guitarist and music minister at local parishes (which she continues to do), plus eighteen years as an instructor for the St. Cloud Diocesan Family Life Bureau. The poetry muse whispered to her in 1989, and she began writing poetry after attending a course in biblio/poetry therapy, taught by Arleen McCarty Hynes, O.S.B., R.P.T., co-author of *Biblio/Poetry Therapy, the Interactive Process: A Handbook*. Currently, Mary works part time with five separate groups as a co-facilitator of poetry therapy in the St. Cloud Hospital's Recovery Plus program for addiction.